CW01501443

The *1619 Project – Part 2* is a research project originally published in Academia.edu. The information presented herein is based on well-documented historical evidence published by respected historians.

ISBN-9798685461971

Front Cover
The Slave Market
Artist: Jean-Leon Gerome 1866
This work is in the public domain.

Back Cover
Photo of Judah P. Benjamin 1856
This work is in the public domain.

The 1619 Project – Part 2
The History of the Slavic Slave Business

John Tuman, Jr.

For Ivan Dosiak

ACKNOWLEDGMENTS

The author is indebted to the hard work of scholars such as Mikhail Kizilov, Alan Fisher, Brian L Davies, Mike Dash, Yaron Ben-Naeh, Michael Khodarkovsky, Eizo Matsuki, Katalin Siska, and others, who have researched the archives of the former Soviet Union and the Ottoman Empire to develop a more comprehensive understanding of the history of the Slavic slave trade. This history needs to be understood, remembered, and presented forcefully, clearly, and honestly to inform and educate the American public.

ABOUT THE AUTHOR

The author has worked alongside his Slavic brothers in the coal mines, steel mills, and sweatshops of Pennsylvania. He has been a worker, a soldier, an engineer, a project manager, consultant, college professor, businessman, and author. He has had a lifelong interest in the history of Eastern Europe and especially of Ukraine. When not engaged in research, travel, and writing, you can find him at his favorite café in the Marais section of Paris.

Introduction

In August 2019, The New York Times Magazine published the "The 1619 Project," a collection of essays on slavery in the United States. The publication received widespread praise as well as extensive criticism from both historians and the public. The New Your Times explained why they published The 1619 Project as follows:

> 1619 is not a year that most Americans know as a notable date in our country's history. Those who do are at most a tiny fraction of those who can tell you that 1776 is the year of our nation's birth. What if, however, we were to tell you that the moment that the country's defining contradictions first came into the world was in late August of 1619? That was when a ship arrived at Point Comfort in the British colony of Virginia, bearing a cargo of 20 to 30 enslaved Africans. Their arrival inaugurated a barbaric system of chattel slavery that would last for the next 250 years. Slavery is sometimes referred to as the country's original sin, but it is more than that: it is the country's very origin.

> Out of slavery — and the anti-black racism it required — grew nearly everything that has truly made America exceptional: its economic might, its industrial power, its electoral system, its diet and popular music, the inequities of its public health and education, its astonishing penchant for violence, its income inequality, the example it sets for the world as a land of freedom and equality, its slang, its legal system and the endemic racial fears and hatreds that continue to plague it to this day. The seeds of all that were planted long before our official birth date, in 1776, when the men known as our founding fathers formally declared independence from Britain.

> The goal of The 1619 Project is to reframe American history by considering what it would mean to regard 1619 as our nation's birth year. Doing so requires us to place the consequences of slavery and the contributions

of black Americans at the very center of the story we tell ourselves about who we are as a country.

All the essays and the 17 literary works in The 1619 Project put the responsibility for slavery in the United States squarely on the shoulders of white Christian Americans. The 1619 Project makes some compelling arguments and some shocking claims. However, what is most surprising is not what is said in all the essays, but what is not said. Nowhere in the 1619 Project is mention made of the people who were most prominent in the slave business for more than 500 years – the Jews.

Was this a conspiracy of silence between the black authors of The 1619 Project and the Jewish owners of the New York Times?

Objectives

In this paper, we will examine the activities of Jews in the slave business over several centuries and across vast geographic areas, and we will discuss in detail the role of Jews in the slave business in America. No discussion of the history of slavery in America can be complete if we ignore Jewish participation and practice of slavery. Furthermore, this is important because as Eli Faber said in his book, "Jews, Slaves, and the Slave Trade":

> Greater knowledge of the role played by Jewish merchants and colonists in the institution of slavery can only enhance our understanding of the development of the Atlantic economy and the emergence of an Atlantic wide perspective in the early modern world.

In this paper, we use the term "slave business" to be all-inclusive; that is, the buying and selling of slaves, the owning of slaves, the management of slaves, the ransoming of slaves, and the supporting and promoting of slavery by word or deed. By our definition, the "slave business" addresses every manner of promotion and exploitation of a subjugated human being

The information presented herein is based on well-documented historical evidence published by respected historians.

Specifically, this paper will:

1. Discuss the role of Ashkenazi Jews in 17th century Poland as leaseholders of Polish manor estates, money lenders, tavern owners, and slave overseers.

2. Review the activities of Rabbanite and Karaite Jews in Crimea as prison guards, slave ransom negotiators, slave owners and slave traders

3. Look at the Sephardic Jews of the Ottoman Empire, and how they operated their guilds to use, buy, sell, and deliver slaves across the Ottoman Empire and even into the Americas

4. Explore the slave business activities of American Jews and how they bought slaves, owned slaves, sold slaves, invested in slave enterprises, and defended the institution of slavery right up to the end of the Civil War

5. Finally, we will discuss why the New York Times 1619 Project failed to address Jewish involvement in slavery.

The goal of this paper is to contribute to the New York Times 1619 Project to help reframe American history in a way that is comprehensive, honest and just.

Chapter 1

17th Century Poland and the Ashkenazi Jews

At the dawn of the 17th century, Poland was a world power; it had defeated the German Teutonic Knights, the Swedes, and the Russians. It formed a union with its neighbor, Lithuania, a smaller but militarily powerful country, to create the Polish-Lithuanian Commonwealth. Poland's combined territories stretched from the Baltic in the north to the Black Sea in the south, and from the Habsburg Empire in the west almost to the gates of Moscow in the east.

Nobles made up about 10% of the population and controlled 90% of the nation's wealth. Every noble had the same standing. Some nobles could be as poor as a peasant and others as rich as a king, yet they all had equal voting power in Poland's parliament, the Sejm.

Only a noble could vote, and for an act to pass, a 100% majority vote was required. Any noble could stop an initiative by voting against it (the liberum veto) or not showing up to vote. However, wealthy nobles could cajole, bribe, or threaten the poorer nobles to support the initiatives they wanted. Polish nobles elected the king. The king had virtually no power, and as it was stated many times, "The King may reign, but the King cannot rule." Even though Poland had some semblance of a democratic system of government, it suffered political gridlock for much of its history.

In the 17th century, the super-rich Polish nobles, the so-called grandees or little kings, ruled Poland. In effect, these nobles were warlords. They owned large sections of the country, they were wealthy, and they had private armies. A typical example of the Polish warlord of that period was

Jeremi Wisniowiecki, who ruled over lands inhabited by 230,000 people and had a private army of 25,000.

These nobles were richer than today's billionaires. Polish families such as the Chortoryisky, Ostrozky, Potocki, Radziwills, Vyshnyvetsky, and Zamoiski owned entire provinces, cities, hundreds of towns and villages, and hundreds of thousands of serfs from which they derived enormous incomes. The Ostrozky estates, for example, generated some ten million guldens per year. These massive holdings were akin to the large plantations of the American South before the Civil War. Farming was the principal business, slaves did all the work, overseers managed the slaves, and the privileged owners controlled everything and became extremely wealthy.

In the year 1619, Europe began to tear itself apart in the Thirty Years' War. Poland stayed out of the conflict and became rich from its grain trade with Europe. Profits from the grain trade motivated Polish nobles to undertake a colonization program in the wild steppes of Ukraine. At that time, Ukraine was the last frontier in Europe, a vast, wild, untamed land, almost deserted except for bandits, runaway slaves, and small communities of hardy Ukrainian settlers.

When the nobles moved in with their troops, administrators, craftsmen, and slaves, they launched a massive land grab. The nobles set out to extract the wealth of the land by any ruthless means. Hence, they seized villages, towns, cities, and vast areas of the Ukrainian wilderness for their own; they constructed castles, walls, roads, bridges, buildings, and mills. Slaves did all the work on the vast estates; they not only toiled in the fields, but they also worked in the quarries, mines, and wherever labor was needed.

The nobles created a vast and complex infrastructure that required administrative and management proficiency. However, instead of creating a large and expensive bureaucracy to manage their estates, the Polish nobles did something clever. They used what they called the Arenda system to lease out their estates to the highest bidder for a fixed fee. The only people with ready cash to bid on these lucrative leases were Jews.

From the earliest recorded history, it is known that Jewish merchants called the Radhaniya, traveled the trade routes from China, Europe, Persia, and elsewhere to export eunuchs, slave girls and boys, brocades, furs, and swords. Thus, for centuries the Jews traveled the world's trade routes buying, selling, lending money, collecting debts, entering into contracts, and keeping records of business transactions. As a result, they built a network of contacts and associates in every country and every major city throughout the known world; they could issue letters of credit to buy, sell or bribe as necessary to organize business ventures that would generate a profit. The Polish nobles needed people with these skills, and they went to great lengths to encourage Jews to migrate to Poland. By the 17th century, Poland had one of the largest Ashkenazi Jewish populations in the world.

For the Ashkenazi Jews, 17th century Poland was the land of opportunity. In most of Europe, Jews lived under oppressive restrictions, but Poland granted freedom and opportunities to its Jewish population. To encourage Jews to immigrate to Poland to help develop its economy, the nobles, as early as 1264, passed decrees allowing Jews to govern themselves by their own laws and customs; in effect, Poland had a government within a government. By law, Poland allowed Jews to lend money, charge interest, and sell alcohol, most unusual for a very Catholic country like Poland. Even though other European countries expelled Jews for usury and the slave-trading of Christians, Poland was indifferent to these practices. In Poland, under the Arenda system, Jews could lease estates from nobles, usually for three years, and run them as their own.

The role of the Jews in 17th century Poland, to paraphrase the Jewish historian Israel Friedlander, was to act as a giant sponge to suck the wealth out of the land and put it into the pockets of the nobles. Of course, the Jews put plenty of money into their own pockets. The source of all that money was slavery.

By definition, a slave is someone whose life is controlled by someone else, i.e., his or her master. Slavery has existed just about everywhere since the beginning of history down to the 19th century. War produced slaves. Prisoners of war were either killed or enslaved. Those with wealth could buy their freedom; the rest were doomed to a life of servitude. Frequently, families traveled with armies; hence, prisoners of war with families taken as slaves would eventually produce offspring that were born into slavery.

In the 17th century, Poland outlawed slavery; however, the law merely gave slaves a new name, "serf." Serfs were the soil-bound peasants who were forced to work for the nobles to earn their daily bread. They could not leave the land, were treated as beasts of burden and were deliberately kept illiterate. Most of the serfs/slaves in Ukraine were Orthodox Christians, and because of the religious bigotry of the Catholic Polish nobles, the serfs/slaves were deprived of their rights and held in contempt.

Both Poles and Jews produced significant written records about the world they lived in, while the illiterate serfs/slaves created an oral history in the form of songs, proverbs, riddles, fairy tales, and oral epics. Both written records and oral traditions make clear that serfs/slaves were the victims of b\ \'al injustice. Under the Arenda system, the ser. \ were systematically exploited, harshly treated, and . \ ' by those in power.

For the Jews, leasing a Polish. \ eman's estate was a high-reward, high-risk undertaking. \ leaseholder could make as much as a 200% return on . \ stment; he could also go bankrupt. Once the leaseholder ix k control of the estate, he, in effect, became the de facto nobleman with all the powers he needed to run the estate as he saw fit to make a profit. For the leaseholder, the challenges were many. First, the serfs/slaves were not inclined to work from sunrise to sunset to enrich their Jewish masters. Also, many natural disasters could drive the leaseholder into bankruptcy; droughts, storms, locusts, poor harvests, and diseases were always present.

So how did the Jewish leaseholder address these challenges? For the reluctant serf/slave workers, there were plenty of strong, brutal overseers who used clubs and whips to keep the serfs/slaves productive. If things got out of hand and slaves revolted, and there were several revolts, the Polish nobles, with their private armies, moved to crush any uprising with great brutality.

In modern times, to address the risk of natural disasters, a business owner can buy insurance; however, these instruments did not exist in the 17th century; hence, the leaseholder did the next best thing. He shared the risk. The leaseholder would subcontract portions of his lease holdings to other Jews.

Thus, other Jews could purchase a subcontract to operate taverns, inns, mills, fishing ponds, woodlands, pasture lands, and anything else that could be taxed. Historical records show that in some districts, Jews would stand in front of the Orthodox Christian church and demand payment from the parishioners before they were allowed to enter. Over time, as the Arenda system expanded across the Polish-Commonwealth, the serfs/slaves would rarely, if ever, see the nobleman who owned the estate, but they would see, daily, a Jew in charge of every facet of their lives.

Opportunities were so good for Jews at that time that they tried to keep other Jews out of Poland. Nevertheless, despite the restrictions that Polish Jews formulated, Jews from all walks of life streamed into Poland; hence, by the 17th century, Poland had the largest population of Jews in Europe, making up about one-fifth of the population of Poland.

The historian Norman Davies reported in his book, "God's Playground: A History of Poland," that the Poland-Lithuanian Commonwealth became "the paradise of the Jews, purgatory for the Burger's and hell for the peasants." The richer Jews openly aspired to a noble lifestyle; they took to wearing swords and gold chains, and not a few were formally ennobled and even affected the noble's habit of not paying taxes. In Ukraine, Jews were widely denounced as a chosen instrument of the Polish lords.

By the 17th century, Jews in the Polish-Lithuanian Commonwealth were firmly entrenched as the moneylenders, alcohol providers, estate-slave overseers, and international slave traders. Using today's vernacular, we would classify these Jews as loan sharks, drug dealers, and slave traders; however, we must keep in mind that in the 17th century, the Jews were not doing anything illegal. However, the Jews and their Polish lords imposed social injustice on oppressed peoples that produced abject poverty, alcoholism, ignorance, and hatred. More than anything else, this social injustice has, to this day, fostered anti-Semitism and mistrust among many Christians.

In many respects, the Arenda system, as fashioned by the Polish nobles, was even more brutal than that of the slave plantations of America's old South. When a plantation owner bought a slave, he made a major capital investment in an instrument of labor. The plantation owner, to protect his investment and ensure a sufficient return, would feed, clothe, and house his slaves to maintain their health and physical well-being so they could be good workers.

For the Jewish leaseholders of the large noble estates, maintaining the well-being of the serfs/slaves was not their concern. The leaseholders did not own the serfs/slaves and were not responsible for their well-being. On the large Polish estates, the serf/slave had to construct his cottage, maintain his gardens to feed his family and care for himself and his family in times of sickness or injury. As far as the Jewish leaseholder was concerned, his goal was to extract as much wealth as possible from the nobleman's estate in the shortest possible time. The Jewish leaseholders did not build hospitals or schools or provide doctors for the serfs/slaves.

Across the entire Polish Lithuanian Empire, the Arenda system gave the Polish nobles and their Jewish leaseholders wealth, privilege, and comfort. At the same time, the estate serfs/slaves were ground down in poverty and despair.

Jews did not work in the fields from sunrise to sundown; hence, they had time for intellectual pursuits and education. Jews placed great emphasis on education. The 17century Jewish historian Nathan Hanover in his book, "Abyss of Despair," reported: "Each community maintains academies, and the head of each Academy was given an ample salary so he could maintain his school without worry...each community maintained young men and provided for them a weekly allowance of money that they might study with the head of the Academy. The boys were provided with food from the community benevolent fund or from the public kitchen."

Indeed, when Jewish boys were in their classrooms, they could look out the window and see the children of the serfs/slaves working alongside their parents. Like the black African slaves on the Southern plantations, the serfs/slaves were kept ignorant by their masters.

A merchant who was touring one of the Jewish schools saw the serf/slave children working in the fields; he asked the head of the Academy, "Do those children working in the fields go to school?" The master of the Academy replied, "No, those are children of the serfs, and their destiny is to work in the fields."

The emphasis on education was inherent in Jewish culture and gave the Jews economic and political advantages over their uneducated serfs and peasants. Centuries later, when Jews immigrated to the United States, their educational advantages would position them for opportunities that were not available to the uneducated or illiterate immigrants to America.

In the 17th century Polish-Lithuanian Commonwealth, the political, legal, and economic advantages enjoyed by Jews enabled them to fashion a lifestyle not unlike the wealthy Polish nobles. In the cities and towns, the Jews lived in well-appointed, large stone houses. Their homes were decorated with elegant furniture, carpeting, tapestry, silver utensils, expensive crockery, and well-stocked kitchens. At the same time, their Christian counterparts lived in, at best, sparsely furnished, small wooden houses. On the manner estates, the Jewish leaseholders had homes that were equivalent to the Polish nobles, while the serfs/slaves lived in thatch-roof huts, slept on straw-covered pallets, and ate out of wooden bowls.

The Polish nobles, to finance their opulent lifestyle, continually put pressure on the Jews to produce more income; the Jews, in turn, forced the serfs/slaves to work longer and harder. Conditions became so brutal that the rabbis pleaded with the Arendars to allow the serfs/slaves one day a week of rest. However, the drive for profits overshadowed any concerns for the lives of the serfs/slaves.

At every opportunity, the serf/slave sought freedom. Like the black slaves in America's old South, Ukrainian serfs ran away. Slaves of the old South fled north to find freedom; Ukrainian serfs sought freedom by fleeing south to join the Cossacks.

Plantation slaves fleeing north might get help from Northern sympathizers by way of the Underground Railroad; however, Ukrainian serfs/slaves fleeing south to join the Cossacks could not count on any help. They traveled hundreds of miles across the Ukrainian steppes facing bandits, Tatar slave raiders, hunger, and severe weather before they reached the Cossack fortress on the Dnieper River.

Nevertheless, over time, thousands of runaway serfs/slaves joined the Cossacks. Eventually, the ranks of Cossacks consisted mainly of runaway slaves who had a deep hatred of their former Jewish masters. A Cossack revolt erupted across the Polish-Lithuanian Empire in 1648, and the former slaves, now Cossacks, attacked the Polish nobles and Jews with a vengeance.

This revolt was the beginning of the end for the great Polish-Lithuanian Empire, and it changed everything for the Polish Jews. Most of the Jews were driven from their comfortable homes, lost their businesses and wealth, and many numbers were killed or taken as slaves. The upheaval of 1648 shocked the Jewish psyche and caused the

Ashkenazi Jews to turn to Messianism and Hasidism. Today most Jews see themselves only as victims of the revolt with no responsibility for the plight of the serfs/slaves.

The Cossack revolt of 1648 was a little known event that changed the map of Europe and world history. The Ukrainian Cossacks were the first people to fight slavery, they were the first to outlaw slavery, and they were the first to claim that every man was equal; their revolt laid the foundation for a free Ukrainian nation.

The history of Poland is almost unknown in the West. Ask any American what he or she knows about Polish history, and they might refer to the Polish patriots who fought in the American Revolution, Kosciuszko and Pulaski. However, many Americans would be shocked to learn that these patriots of the American Revolution represented a class of people, the nobles, whose wealth was based on the blood and sweat of oppressed serfs/slaves.

Chapter 2

17th Century Crimea and the Rabbanite and Karaite Jews

In the 13th century, Genghis Khan's Mongolian hordes swept into Europe, destroying everything in their path. For the next 200 years, the Mongols collected tribute from their conquered nations and maintained law and order with an iron fist. Eventually, the Mongol Empire fragmented as the different tribes settled into various conquered lands. The remnants of the Golden Horde, the Tatars who had conquered Russia, settled comfortably in Crimea and became the Khanate of Crimea. For the next 200 years, the Khanate attacked Russia, Poland, and Ukraine to capture slaves by the tens of thousands every year.

Since we do not teach Polish, Russian or Turkish history in American schools, Tatar raids and the slavery of Christians are virtually unknown to most Americans. However, it is a fact that this slavery is older, larger, and more brutal than the African slave trade to America. As the historian Mike Dash in his paper, "Blond Cargo: Finnish children in the slave markets of medieval Crimea," put it:

> When we think of slavery, we tend to think of this African traffic. Yet it was not the only such trade – nor was it, before 1700, even the largest. A second great market in slaves once sullied the world, this one less well-known, vastly longer-lasting, and centered on the Black Sea ports of the Crimea. It was a huge trade in its own right; in its great years, which roughly lasted from 1200 until 1760, an estimated 6.5 million captives were shipped off to and often intensely miserable lives in places ranging from Italy to India.

Slavery in the Crimea, however, differed in significant ways from the trans-Atlantic trade. The slaves sold there were white, being drawn from for the most part from the Great Plains of Ukraine and southern Russia in annual raids known as the "harvesting of the steppe.

Most of the slaves were not male laborers. They were women and children destined for domestic service – a fate that not infrequently included sexual service.

More women than men were sold in the Crimea, and they consistently fetched higher prices. Female slaves were twice as expensive as males. As a result, as many as 80% of all Black Sea slaves whose sexes and ages are known were females aged between 8 and 24.

As Mike Dash reported, "The most prized of all variety of slaves, however, appear to have been children brought to Crimea from the far north – boys and girls who were perhaps between six and 13 years old, who had been seized in organized raids on the Finnish district of Karelia and then trafficked via Novgorod, Moscow and the Volga."

The size and the scope of the Tatar raids were almost unimaginable. For example, in the 16th century, Tatar armies burned much of Moscow, killing upwards of 80,000 and carrying off some 150,000 captives. A French engineer, Guillaume Beauplan, stationed with the Polish Army in Ukraine, estimated that Tatar armies could be as large as 80,000, but a typical invasion force would probably average about 30,000 warriors.

A Tatar army of 30,000 or more warriors, with some 90,000 horses, and riding 10 to 12 abreast in a column several miles long, hurrying across the steppes, must have been an awesome and terrifying sight. Downwind of the Tatars, one could see the cloud of dust and smell the unwashed bodies of thousands of men and animals.

The Tatars had seven main invasion trails from Crimea into the Muscovy and Polish-Lithuanian lands. All the invasions began at the narrow fortified Isthmus of Perekop, where the Crimean Peninsula joins the mainland. Most Crimean Tatar invasions were planned for harvest time so the army could forage and plunder for several weeks. There were also shorter incursions in early winter when the rivers had frozen over, and there was sufficient snow on the ground to keep their horses' unshod hooves from cracking from the frost.

The Crimean Khan would issue a *ghaza*, a summons for a religious war. Every able-bodied male over the age of 15 was ordered to report with three horses, food, and weapons for an invasion of Slavic lands.

Tatar warriors carried a short reflex bow, a quiver of 20 to 30 arrows, a saber, and a lance. Wealthy Tatars might wear chain mail and an iron helmet; for food, the Tatar warriors packed a few pounds of roasted millet, bread, and some cooked meats. The loot they took from captured villages would satisfy the bulk of their needs.

The average Tatar was short, barely 5 feet tall; a wealthy noble who had a better diet might be slightly taller. They had swarthy complexions, round heads, flat faces, and distinctive Asian features. Most Tatars dressed in sheepskin and homespun cloth.

The Crimean Tatars were excellent horsemen. They set their stirrups high, used whips instead of spurs to control their horses, and fired arrows from their compound bows at a rapid rate with deadly accuracy, all the while riding at full gallop. They traveled in columns a dozen riders wide. Depending on the size of the army, a column could be several miles long.

The Tatar army would assemble at Perekop and take one of seven trails into Slavic lands. Experienced warriors knew the trails well and would employ tactics that enabled them to harvest slaves with minimal risk wherever possible. They avoided combat with Polish or Russian forces and, in particular, the Zaporozhian Ukrainian Cossacks. They sought easy targets; small villages, poorly defended towns or cities, farmers working in the fields, men fishing on the lakes and rivers, and traders traveling in small groups. Their goal was to minimize risks, avoid casualties, and maximize profit. They sought healthy young females, strong males, young children, and even infants. The young brought the highest prices in the slave markets of the Muslim world. The Tatars also took horses, cattle, sheep, wagons, weapons, tools, grain, seed, and anything else of value from captured villages, towns, or cities. When the Tatars finished looting, they burned all the houses and buildings to the ground.

Captives had their hands tied behind their backs and ropes lashed around their necks. The Tatars lined up all the captives and coupled them together with wooden poles and forced them to walk in long lines, with mounted Tatar warriors riding along on both sides. Captives had to walk hundreds of miles before they got to the Tatar prisons in Crimea. The great mass of mounted warriors, prisoners, wagons, and livestock could be several miles long. The mounted Tatar guards used their whips to keep the prisoners moving, and anyone who could not keep up, the wounded, the sick, the lame, or the old, was cut down by Tatar sabers. Years later, the route traveled by the Tatar raiders would still be evident by the broken wagons, trash, and bleached bones of animals, men, women, and children.

As Mikhail Kizilov reported in his paper, "Slaves, Money Lenders, and Prison Guards: The Jews and the Trade in Slaves and Captives in the Crimean Khanate."

Trade in slaves and captives was one of the most important (if not the most important) sources of income of the Crimean Khanate in the sixteenth to eighteenth centuries. According to some estimates, in the first half of the seventeenth century, about 150,000 to 200,000 captives were taken to the Crimea. The number of captives transported by the Crimean Tatar from Poland-Lithuania and Russia (not including the Caucasus) approached 10,000 per annum, which is two million for the period between 1500 and 1700. Thus, the Black Sea slave trade was fully comparable in size with the Atlantic slave trade of the same period (ca. two million between 1451 and 1600) and declined only in the 18th century.

Some believe that the number of captives taken by the Crimean Tatars was higher than that of the Atlantic slave trade; however, it is almost impossible to get an accurate estimate of the size of the Black Sea slave trade. The historian Alan Fisher, who has studied the history of Crimea in detail, attempted to determine the number of slaves involved during this period. Still, he found it impossible to get any reliable answers.

When the Tatar armies completed their raids, they returned to Perekop and passed through the main gate of the fortress that protected the Crimean Peninsula. Customs officials at the gate were responsible for counting the harvest of slaves and loot. With as many as 30,000 men, women, and children captives and hundreds if not thousands of sheep, cattle, horses, and wagons, it would take the custom officials and staff most of the day to give the Khan an accurate accounting of the results of his raid. This accounting was necessary because the Khan was responsible for making an equitable distribution of the loot to his troops. He also had to pay a customs fee of some 10%.

Once inside, the Crimean-mainland Tatars selected the slaves and loot they wanted, and then sold the rest to Jewish merchants who lived in Crimea.

Before 1475, it was mainly Italian (Genoese) merchants who transported large numbers of captives from Kafka to Genoa or other ports. However, after the Ottomans captured Constantinople and took control of Crimea, the Genoese were thrown out of Crimea, and Rabbanite and Karaite Jews became the dominant force in the slave business.

Numerous European sources tell us about Jewish slave traders as early as the 10th century. From the 13th century onwards, the Crimean Jewish population was divided into two distinctive groups: the non-Talmudic Karaite Jews and the Rabbanite Jews, who followed the Talmud. These religious differences notwithstanding, both groups soon adopted the language and everyday customs of their Turkic-speaking Tatar neighbors. The Jews, being skillful and cunning merchants, took an active part in the slave trade as slave owners, traders, guards, and mediators in the ransoming of slaves.

Tatars took their slaves to Crimean dungeons, where the slaves were classified according to age, sex, and skills. They were then inspected for physical appearance or defects. Sometimes male prisoners would be castrated and branded. This brutal treatment of slaves by the Crimean Tatars is well documented.

The fate of the slaves depended on their masters. Christian sources are full of descriptions of the suffering of Christian slaves captured by the Crimean Tatars; for example, Mikhail Kizilov, in his paper, "Slave trade in the Early Modern Crimea from the Perspective of Christian, Muslim, and Jewish sources," states:

Among these unfortunates there are many strong ones if they the Tatars have not castrated them yet, cut off their ears and nostrils, burned cheeks and foreheads with the burning iron, they force them to work with their chains and shackles during the daylight and sit in prison during the night; they are sustained by the meager food consisting of dead animals meat, rotten, full of worms, which even the dog would not eat. The youngest women are kept for their pleasure.

Old men and children were usually given to be tortured by the young Tatars so that the latter would learn how to kill as if the hunters gave partridges to be torn to pieces by the young Falcons. One Crimean Muslim author mentioned that after one raid, each Tatar soldier killed about 10 to 15 captives for his own amusement.

Captive men that the Tatars did not kill were put to work in the fields; Tatars seldom cultivated the soil themselves. The captives, now slaves, worked from sunup to sundown to do all the heavy agricultural work needed to make the Tatar fields productive; they plowed the fields, sowed the seeds, cultivated the crops, harvested the hay and wheat, and took care of the cattle and sheep. The slaves suffered greatly from lack of water and food; their daily meal generally consisted of a piece of black bread and a plate of grated cabbage with salt. Soon their clothes completely disintegrated; they were burned continuously by the sun and covered by mud. Hence, most slaves lived seminude, with rags or sheepskin covering their bodies.

Female slaves taken by Tatars fared much better than males. Most of the female slaves worked as household servants or concubines for their Tatar masters. Some authors reported that Crimean Tatars took foreign female slaves as wives because of the rather ugly appearance of Tatar women.

After the Tatars selected the slaves they wanted, the rest would be sold to the Jews. Both the Rabbanite and Karaite Jews bought female slaves to work as household servants and for sexual purposes. The male slaves they bought were put to work in their fields, shops, or warehouses.

However, most of the men and women slaves the Jews bought were sold across the Ottoman Empire. Strong, healthy Slavic males were sold to work in the fields, in the mines, on the construction of walls, roads, and buildings, or to row on a galley slave ship.

Indeed, the worst fate for captive male slaves was to be sold as a galley slave to the Ottoman Turks. The Ottoman government purchased the largest number of slaves shipped from the Black Sea to Istanbul for their galleys. For example, in 1576, the Ottoman navy purchased 6000 slaves to staff 20 galleys, and in 1590 they purchased 4000 more, and they continued to buy Slavic slaves to man their galleys well into the 17th century. Usually, only Russian slaves were used on Ottoman galleys. Since the mortality rate of galley slaves was high, the continuous supply of new slaves from abroad was indispensable to the Ottoman government.

Life for the African slaves who worked on America's Southern plantations and in sugar factories was brutal; however, this brutality paled in comparison to that of a Slavic rower on an Ottoman galley.

A typical Ottoman galley was long and narrow and had two large sails and hundreds of rowers. The rowers sat on narrow benches on each side of the ship; a long wooden runway located slightly above the rowers' shoulders extended the length of the ship. Overseers walked back and forth on the runway to ensure that each slave worked hard rowing; a sharp crack of the whip to a man's back motivated any slacker. A timekeeper sat at the end of the runway and beat the drum to set the pace for the rowers.

While at sea, the rowers lived on their benches. They were chained to their bench and wore only a loincloth; they ate, drank, slept, urinated, and defecated where they sat. Human waste and garbage dropped below their feet; the stench assailed the nostrils, the eyes, and the sensibilities of every nerve in a man's body; even animals would not live in the kind of filth that existed in a slave ship. Once a day, rowers were fed two very hard, twice-baked biscuits and a cup of water; hunger and thirst constantly gnawed at every fiber of a rower's body.

When in port, a slave ship was moved to shallow water and drain valves opened to let seawater flow into the bottom of the ship. The ship was then sunk in the shallow water so the slaves could flush out the human waste and garbage. After cleaning the ship, they closed the drain valves, pumped out the water, and floated it back to the dock. While in port, the slaves were in a prison or dungeon. The average life of a galley slave was 3 to 5 years.

However, for the Rabbanite and Karaite Jews, it was young boys and young girls that offered the most profit potential. The Jewish slave traders would categorize the children by age, appearance, and fitness.

Attractive girls were sent to the Sultan's harems, others were destined to be concubines for wealthy merchants, and others to work in the soldiers' brothels. Plain girls would work as household servants or laborers in Ottoman factories or shops.

Boys of robust stature would be selected to be slave soldiers in the Ottoman's elite armies, the Janissaries, or the Egyptian Mamluk. Other boys, fair in appearance and slight in build, would be castrated to become eunuchs to work in the Sultan's harem, or as clerks and administrators in Ottoman officials' homes or offices.

Castrating young boys to provide eunuchs to the Ottoman Turks was a highly profitable business. The brutality of this procedure is difficult to comprehend in modern times. Still, it is necessary to describe the process, to fully understand the cruelty, the pain, and the suffering that was inflicted on these young Slavic boys.

The doctor, probably a Karaite, would direct his staff to prepare the young boys for castration. Each boy was put on a narrow board and tied so he could not move or twitch. Ropes bound his ankles, thighs, chest, and arms. The young boys would lay there, eyes wide open, faces contorted by fear, crying out for their mothers; they knew what was about to happen. The doctor would sit at a long table, and his assistants would put the bound boys, one at a time in quick succession, on the table in front of him. The doctor would pay no attention to the crying boys; he performed so many castrations that he was impervious to their screams and pleas. He held a sharp curved knife in his right hand, grabbed the boy's organs with his left hand, and with a single swipe of his right-hand slice the organ in one quick snap of the wrist. Their little bodies jerked, contracted, and froze as pain exploded through every nerve; their screams, cries, tears, and appeals to mother and God would echo to the building. The shock killed some boys on the spot; others might suffer in agony for days and then die of infection. Castrated boys lay crying and whimpering like puppies.

Those that endured the agony and recovered were shipped to their new masters. More than two-thirds of the slaves sold in Crimea were sent to the Ottoman capital, a voyage of about ten days. Once in the capital, Ottoman government officials would select the slaves they wanted, and the Jewish slave-traders' guild would purchase the rest.

The Tatars also generated considerable income through the ransoming of slaves. Polish and Russian nobles, wealthy businessmen, and other people of means could buy their freedom. Prominent figures such as the Polish nobles Potocki and Kalinowski and the Cossack Hetman Bohdan Khmelnytsky spent time in Tatar prisons until they eventually purchased their freedom.

The ransoming process could take considerable time, and in most cases, it was the Rabbanite and Karaite Jews who acted as intermediaries between the parties and conducted the negotiations for the release of the prisoners.

For the Jews, this must have been a very profitable activity because we have examples of Jews who traveled hundreds of miles across dangerous lands to conduct these negotiations. In one documented case, a Jewish merchant, Arslan, traveled from Crimea to Sweden; however, the records indicate that many of these negotiations were carried out in Crimea, Poland, or Moscow with the Czar and Russian nobles.

Ransoming of slaves was an unusually heavy financial burden on Moscow. The Czar had to impose an annual tax on all residents of his empire to help offset the cost of the ransoming of Russian citizens.

In the 17th century, Russia had the almost impossible task of defending its vast empire; therefore, the Tatars ravaged Russian lands well into the 18th century. Russia spent considerable time and money establishing frontier communities to defend their territories. They even built a defensive wall, known as the Belgorod line, a chain of fortified settlements connected with earth ramparts and long lines of felled trees. This defensive line eventually ran for some 800 km and was successful in limiting the Tatars' freedom of movement and helped somewhat to eliminate large-scale raids by the 1760s.

Many scholars believe that the drain on Russia's resources to fend off Tatar raids and the ransoming of their citizens was one of the reasons that Russia lagged behind Western Europe for many centuries. Much of this history is unknown to Western readers; however, those who are interested in learning more should read two important works: "Warfare, State and Society on the Black Sea Steppes, 1500 – 1700," by Brian L Davies, and "Russia's Steppes Frontier, the Making of a Colonial Empire, 1500 – 1800," by Michael Khodarkovsky.

In addition to being mediators and negotiators for the ransoming of slaves, Jews also functioned as moneylenders to families involved in the ransom process of loved ones. Jews also provided financial support to foreign diplomats living in Crimea.

Indeed, Jews functioned as slave traders, ransom negotiators, and moneylenders, which fit well with their culture as merchants and entrepreneurs. Somewhat surprisingly, however, is that records indicate that Jews also served as slave prison guards and prison administrators for the Tatars in Crimea. The records also show that Cufut-Qal'eh (Turk. "Jewish fortress"), was a medieval Crimean town where numerous and influential Karaites lived up to the annexation of Crimea in 1783. Tatar officials regularly used this town as a place for housing important and significant prisoners. Karaite Jews functioned as the commandants, garrison guards, and gatekeepers of the prison.

With the opening of government archives in Russia, Poland, and Turkey in the 1980s, and the hard work of scholars such as Mikhail Kizilov, Alan Fisher, Mike Dash, Yaron Ben-Naeh, Eizo Matsuki, Katalin Siska, and others, we are finally getting a better understanding of the extent and the cruelty of the Ottoman slave trade and the role of Jews in this business. Especially within the last decade, scholars in America, Eastern Europe, and Turkey have published many research papers dealing with the Ottoman slave trade; these papers are available on academia.edu. Also, many scholarly works are presented at the World Congress of Jewish studies held annually in Jerusalem.

Much of what we know about the lives of Karaite and Rabbanite Jews in the Crimean slave business is summarized by Mikhail Kizilov in the conclusion of his paper, "Slaves, Moneylenders, and Prison Guards: The Jews and the Trade in Slaves and Captives in a Crimean Khanate," as follows:

> As has been demonstrated in the article, despite their fragmentary character, the sources allow reconstructing a general picture of Jewish involvement into the Crimean trade in slaves and captives. Moreover, they allow developing an absolutely new perspective on the role of Jewish populations in the history of the Crimean Khanate. The sources testify that Jewish population played a highly significant role in the trade in slaves and captives of the Crimean Khanate the 16th to 18th centuries. The ways in which the Jews were engaged in this business, were varied and diversified – from mediators in trade and moneylenders to commandants of the Jewish fortress of Cufut-Qal'eh, from wealthy slave-owners to misfortunate victims of the Tatar predatory raids. Moreover the Jews played an important role in the international trade and were sometimes appointed influential state officials of the Crimean Khanate. A Jewish merchant was highly important for those who wanted to redeem the relatives at a lesser price than that was offered by Tatar officials (see the testimony of Martins Broniovius). A Jewish merchant could also be sent to solve financial matters of important captives as

far as Sweden (e.g., the case of the Jewish merchant Arslan); he could purchase captives to use them as his domestic or sell them to Jewish merchants from other countries. A Jew could also be commandant of the whole mountainous fortress housing important prisoners belonging to the Tatar Khans (e.g., the Karaite <u>qapuct</u> Saltik). Nevertheless, the Jews themselves could also become victims of Tatar slavers.

Chapter 3

17th Century Ottoman Empire and the Sephardic Jews

In 1452 the Muslin Sultan, Mehmet II, mobilized a vast army of 80,000 to 200,000 men and a fleet of some 320 ships to attack the city of Constantinople. At this time, Constantinople was just a shadow of its former self. In 1204, the city was looted by the Christian armies of the fourth Crusade; later, the Black Plague decimated its population. Nevertheless, the small Christian Imperial Army of about 7000 held off one Turkish assault after another. Mehmet made one final attack in three waves and stormed into the city. Emperor Constantine fought hand-to-hand with his troops and was killed; his body was never found.

Sultan Mehmet II's conquest of Constantinople on May 29, 1453 ended the thousand-year reign of the Roman Empire and changed the course of Western history. The Sultan was a gifted leader and a visionary, so he decided to move the Ottoman capital from Edirne to Constantinople to position himself for future conquests in Europe.

Mehmet quickly set about rebuilding Constantinople and offered incentives to merchants and artisans to move into the city. In short order, Greek, Armenians, and Jews came to the city and initiated business and commercial activities that enabled the Ottoman Empire to grow, thrive, and become a world power that would endure for the next 400 years.

All non-Muslim residents of the Ottoman Empire were classified as dhimmi, which meant that they had an inferior status and hence, had to pay a head tax and live under certain restrictions concerning dress and behaviors. For example, religious services could not be conducted in public spaces, Christian church bells were forbidden, and Christians were called to services by drums. In Constantinople, Byzantine churches had been converted to mosques by the early 16th century. In reality, most of these restrictions were mild, and the Greek, Armenian, Jews, and others thrived under Ottoman rule. By far, the Jews fared better than all the other non-Muslim populations in the Ottoman Empire.

Jews had a long history of international entrepreneurship, business, and finance, and had contacts and associates across the Muslim and Christian world. For the most part, the Muslim Turks were disinterested in business and left those activities to the minority religions. Since the Turks were frequently engaged in military conflicts with the Christians, they tended to favor the Jews as being more trustworthy and reliable. Hence, the Jewish people were allowed to establish their autonomous communities, which included their schools and courts, much like the privileges Jews had enjoyed in the Polish-Lithuanian Commonwealth before the takeover by the Russians.

From the early 16th century, the Jewish community in the Ottoman Empire became the largest in the world, and about 90% of Ottoman Jews were Sephardic. The expulsion of Sephardic Jews from Spain and Portugal in the 15th century drove most of the Sephardic Jews to the Ottoman Empire. Many of these Jews were financiers and bankers and had come to the Ottoman Empire not only with expertise in finance but also with hard cash that they used to invest in enterprises across the Ottoman Empire. For example, the banker Alvaro Mendez reportedly brought with him 85,000 gold ducats. The Mendez family soon acquired a dominant position in the state finances of the Ottoman Empire and commerce with Europe.

Revenue-generating enterprises for the Ottoman Empire came from three primary sources: spices, silks, and slaves. Of these three enterprises, the slave business would become the largest, generating upwards to 50% of the taxes and duties paid to the Ottoman government. From the 15th to the 18th century, more than 3 million Christian slaves were sold across the markets of the Ottoman Empire. Most of the Christian slaves came from Rabbanite and Karaite slave traders in Crimea; however, Barbary Coast pirates also harvested slaves from Mediterranean cities and towns.

Captives were sent to Constantinople where the Ottoman government selected the slaves they wanted. The Ottomans had a well-developed process for managing a large number of slaves. First, they identified and classified the slaves; then, they inspected and documented their physical features; from this, they determined their future service. For example, young boys brought from the Balkans and Anatolia might be selected for the Janissaries or government posts. The strongest and most robust boys would go to the military while the best-looking and intelligent boys were trained for administrative positions. They evaluated young girls to determine if they should go to concubines, harems, brothels, or to be housemaids or factory workers.

Older men with skills such as carpenters, masons, or metalworkers were selected to work on construction or factory projects. Unskilled men would work as laborers for the Ottoman navy or army, and older women might become nursemaids caring for young children. The Ottomans kept detailed records of the acquisition cost and the desired selling price of each slave. Each slave sold must produce profit for the Empire.

The captives that the Ottoman government did not want were sold to the slave-trader guilds.

In Constantinople as well as in other Ottoman cities, a specific area was set aside for the slave market. In these markets, Sephardic Jews and others had bought and sold slaves for over 400 years. By far, the largest of these slave-trader guilds belonged to the Sephardic Jews and consisted of some 2000 Sephardic bankers, moneylenders, and merchants. The slave-trader guilds ensured that Jewish traders were not in competition with each other; the guild worked to control prices and minimize competition from other traders. Its goal was to buy slaves at the best price and sell them across the Ottoman Empire at a profit.

The historian Alan Fisher has recorded many eyewitness accounts from visitors to Constantinople of the operation of the slave market. The following is typical of these descriptions:

Slaves were housed in a large building next to a raised platform or stage. Prospective buyers sat or stood in front of the stage to view the slaves that were brought out for sale.

The slave master brought out a family, a sturdy middle-aged man, his wife, and five young children, three boys, and two very young girls. Several buyers stepped forward to examine the children. Two of the buyers were interested in the boys; another buyer wanted the girls for a family that was grieving the loss of their children. Still, another buyer examined the husband and decided that he would make a good worker on one of his farms. None of the buyers were interested in the wife. As the buyers took away the children, the woman got down on her knees, screaming and crying. The husband turned briefly to look at his wife, and then they took him away. The slave master took the wife from the stage and brought out the next group of slaves.

This heartbreaking scene was repeated over and over again until slavery ended in the Ottoman Empire in the 19th century.

Some of the Jewish guild members bought female slaves and took them to their homes to train them to be servants in a Jewish household. Thus, they would teach their Slavic female captives household chores like cooking and embroidery, and the Jewish dietary laws of *kashrut*. A well-trained female slave could command a premier price.

The question one might ask is why did the Ottoman Empire need so many slaves? It is clear that the Ottoman Empire could have never reached the height of the power it enjoyed without slaves. Male slaves were the lifeblood of Ottoman cities, and it's military. In Constantinople, hundreds of slaves worked on the docks loading and unloading cargo from ships in the harbor. As Prof. Kenneth W. Harl of Tulane University reported: "Each year, fleets of cargo ships departed from Sinop, Samsun, and Trabzon to purchase grain for the capital. In 1550, Constantinople's wheat requirements were 73,000 tons (200 tons per day)." Grain and other items from the ships were transported to warehouses and distribution centers all across the city.

Slaves also maintained the infrastructure of the city. The streets had to be swept clean, the garbage and animal waste picked up, and the human waste from cesspools and septic tanks had to be collected and disposed of. In addition, slaves maintained roads and bridges and worked on construction projects and in weapons factories. The Ottomans manufactured swords, lances, firearms, cannons, as well as gunpowder. Slaves, chained to their workbenches, made weapons from sunup to sundown under the watchful eyes of overseers and artisans. Additionally, the Ottoman government had an extensive shipbuilding program, and slaves did much of this work.

The Ottoman military depended heavily on slave labor; as was mentioned before, Slavic Christian slaves manned the galleys of the Ottoman navy. At its height, the Ottoman Empire had hundreds of warships, cargo, and transport ships that required tens of thousands of enslaved oarsmen. The slaves lived under inhumane conditions and received no medical aid. When they were sick, hurt, or worn out, they were thrown overboard.

It was the Ottoman army that probably used more slaves than anyone else. Military historians tend to focus on strategy, tactics, and weapons when they study the successes and failures of an army. They rarely, if ever, consider the role of an army's support personnel (slaves) in determining victory or defeat.

The Ottoman military was unbelievably successful as Prof. Kenneth W. Harl of Tulane University reported:

In the first 400 years of Ottoman history, 1300-1700, an Ottoman Sultan was only defeated decisively twice in a great battle: Angora (on July 20, 1402) and Zenta (on September 11, 1697). In each case, the Sultan had the ill fortune to fight against one of the great captains of history: Tamerlane and Prince Eugene of Savoy.

A significant component of Ottoman military victory was meticulous and detailed planning for supply and logistics, all of which were carried out by a large slave auxiliary army. A reasonable estimate is that for every combat soldier, there were at least 30 or more slaves in support.

Slaves were responsible for moving and transporting the enormous quantity of food, equipment, and munitions needed by the army. Thousands of slaves were required to move the large siege guns that the Ottomans used against enemy fortifications.

When the army was on the move, slaves would set up camp, cook meals, provide clean water, dig wells if needed, take care of the animals, clean up garbage and human and animal waste, and pack and move everything and then do it over again the next day.

During battles and sieges, slaves dug trenches and tunnels and built mounds, ramps, walls, and siege towers. Slaves carried dirt, rocks, reeds, and logs while under fire to fill moats and ditches surrounding castles and cities. Slaves rescue the wounded from the battlefield, provide medical aid, and buried the dead.

During especially difficult sieges, like the assault on the Christian Hospitallers on the island of Malta, slaves were worked to death trying to dig tunnels through solid rock. The Ottoman army could not have achieved the military success it enjoyed without the extensive slave support system it created.

While male slaves lived a life of brutal physical labor, female slaves faced a different fate. Regardless of where in the Ottoman Empire a female captive was sent, she was destined to be primarily a household servant and a sex provider.

Since the founding of Islam, Muslims were permitted to own up to four wives and a harem as large as they could afford. Across the Ottoman Empire, Muslims supplied their households and harems with female slaves captured from Slavic countries. Indeed, owning household slaves and maintaining concubines was expensive and, in a sense, was a testament to the wealth of the owner.

By the 17th century, Jews across the Ottoman Empire, and especially Sephardic Jews living in Constantinople, became the wealthiest of all the minorities living in the Empire. The Jewish population could easily enter into trade with Christian Europe and take advantage of their worldwide network of family connections and knowledge of European affairs to protect their communities, their interests, and to build wealth.

Acting as merchants, moneylenders, and slave traders, the Sephardic Jews obtained prestige and prominence among the Muslim elites. As a result, Jews adopted much of the material life and aesthetics of the Ottoman classes. They built homes that were modest on the outside but richly decorated on the inside; however, they were careful not to project an exaggerated lifestyle that would offend their Muslim neighbors. In Constantinople, Jews were active in music and the performing arts and set the standards for taste and fashion, furniture, and decorative arts.

To a large extent, these wealthy Jews became inculcated with the mores and values of their Muslim neighbors. Both Jewish and Muslim sources make it clear that slave-owning was a status symbol for the middle and upper classes. Hence, successful Jews strived to own slaves.

Initially, non-Muslims were forbidden to own slaves; however, Jews often circumvented this restriction by the use of Muslim intermediaries. Eventually, the Ottomans changed this policy, and Jews and other minorities were permitted to own slaves in return for the payment of a special tax, which was in addition to the poll tax paid by the dhimmi. Slaves in a Jewish household presented several serious problems as discussed by Yaron Ben-Nash of the Hebrew University, Jerusalem, Israel, in his paper, "Blond, tall, with honey-colored eyes: Jewish ownership of slaves in the Ottoman Empire."

> The presence of non-Jewish slaves in Jewish households posed halachic problems, especially when dealing with food. Was the food the slaves touched, even accidentally and especially wine, still kosher? Moreover,

what about the work slaves performed on the Sabbath? The legitimization of the legal offspring was especially thorny. The obvious solution, to convert the slaves, was not free of contradictions: the slave could touch and prepare all food, but he or she could not be made to work on the Sabbath. Apparently, most Jews preferred not to convert slaves even though, at times, this was against the expressed explicit wishes of the latter.

Sexual relations with female slaves was a particularly acute problem. Distinct from Islam, which gave slave owners the right to sexual intercourse with a female slave whose offspring also belonged to him and were considered legitimate heirs, Judaism tends to prohibit this practice, at least "before the fact." Maimonides had already ruled that a man engaged in a sexual relationship with his slave must free her and marry her as a convert to Judaism – or send her away from the household. Much of the reason for this prohibition was the prevention of halachic infractions, first, of the rule against cohabitating with a non-Jewish woman, and second, the law of menstrual separation.

Cohabitation with slaves had not only become somewhat common, but the general Jewish population considered it acceptable.

The sources offer two justifications for ignoring earlier prohibitions: the female slave was bought with "my" money, and I am permitted to do whatever I want with her, the price of payment was also her "marriage price."

For example, in one case: Reuven bought a female servant from Simon, who immersed [in the ritual bath]. He bought her for the purpose of slavery, and it was obvious that he intended to fornicate with her so much so that malicious rumors spread about that he was indeed fornicating with her. The rumors spread throughout the city, and Reuven, for his part, unashamedly admitted to this action, even boasting that he lay with her whenever he wished, and no one could tell him what to do because he bought her with his own money.

The offense itself was a common one. However, on the whole, halachic authorities seem to have resigned themselves to reality, and they limited themselves to condemnations, prescribing mild punishments, if at all. No doubt, they understood that to decree harsh punishment would be to issue rulings with which the "public could not – nor would not – abide." It would be extremely difficult to prevent Jews from doing what was so widely accepted by Islamic urban culture as socially legitimate.

Both Jewish and Muslim sources make it clear that slave-owning was a status symbol for the middle and upper classes. It was also a precondition for managing a respectable household properly.

Slave women may have made peace with their condition precisely in the expectation of freedom and an eventual match. They could at least hope, while in slavery, for eventual ameliorated economic and physical conditions (especially during old-age or sickness).

It is assumed that relations between a married master and a female slave were ruinous: the very presence of a young – and accessible – woman in a household had to have created tensions that would have disturbed normal family equilibrium, especially between husband and wife.

For the wife, the rules of a patriarchal society obliged her to obey her husband. Under these circumstances, she perhaps was even pleased by the help she received in providing for his sexual needs. Also, a slave – concubine, however distasteful, was probably far preferable to the truly frightening prospect of a second or even a third wife, which for Jews under the Ottoman rule was still possible. The legal and socially inferior status of a female slave could not threaten the lady of the house who was protected by a traditional legal mechanism that made it difficult for the husband to divorce her.

For males, sexual liaison with slaves provided a

combination of a convenient, generally socially acceptable (if not halachically), perhaps even a respectable, ongoing relationship with a seemingly inferior woman and a stranger, but nevertheless attractive from many aspects. Thus, the male was able to circumvent the practical injunctions against taking a second wife. The husband – actually, every male – could take up with any woman he chose according to his personal inclinations and taste (beauty probably played a greater role then we may assume), without the need to receive either dispensation from his vow not to marry another or to comply with the venerable, yet still problematic, Jewish ban against bigamy.

It may also have been a comfort to the husband as well as wives that this woman did not threaten the wife's legal status. The slave furthermore was always available and uncompromisingly obedient – she had to be, in fact, since sexual relations were considered a slave's domestic duty. Resisting or lodging complaints would have been fruitless as well as folly. Nor was her upkeep great, which was essentially limited to her daily needs. In addition, lacking a family that might intervene and defend her was another advantage; she could easily be removed from the household without a writ of divorce and without the considerable financial compensation one would owe a true wife.

Ottoman Jews engaged in slave-owning for the same reasons that their Muslim contemporaries did: prestige, sexual fulfillment, and obedient domestic help. Jewish slaveholding is thus an important signifier of acculturation. The blurring of relationships observed in a family where slaves were present may also have been encouraged as a way of downplaying halachic objections, a way, that is, for owners to persuade themselves that what they were engaged in was not "fornication but appropriate family activity.

As we shall see later, these attitudes and beliefs were carried by Jews to the New World.

Slavery in the Ottoman Empire was a legal and significant part of the Ottoman Empire's economy and society, even after several measures to ban slavery in the 19th century failed. The practice continued largely unabated into the early 20th century. As late as 1908, female slaves were still sold in the Ottoman Empire. Sexual slavery was a central part of the Ottoman slave system throughout the history of the institution.

Chapter 4

17th Century American Jews

Jews have been in America as early as 1654, when Sephardic Jews from Brazil settled in the Dutch colony of New Amsterdam, later named New York. These early Jewish immigrants were merchants, entrepreneurs, and slave traders. The Sephardic Jews from Portugal and Spain were active in the slave trade across the Ottoman Empire, the British Colonies, and especially in Brazil.

Over its history, Brazil received more African slaves than any other country, and by the 1800s, almost 50% of the population were slaves. Brazil was the last country in the Western world to end slavery.

It has been recorded that British privateers captured black slaves from Portuguese Sephardic slave ships and brought them to America in 1619. Sephardic Jews had a long connection to the slave trade in the Americas by way of the Jewish slave-traders' guild in Constantinople and the slave markets in America's antebellum South.

The earliest Jewish settlers in New York and Charleston, South Carolina, owned slaves along with other Americans, and Jewish ownership of slaves in America is well documented. An article in "My Jewish Learning," titled *Jews and the African Slave Trade*," posed the question: Did Jews really own slaves? The article answered as follows:

Yes. Jacob Rader Marcus, a historian, and Reform rabbi, wrote in his four-volume history of American Jews that over 75% of Jewish families in Charleston, South Carolina, Richmond, Virginia, and Savannah, Georgia owned slaves, and nearly 40% of Jewish households across the country did. The Jewish population in the cities was quite small, so the total number of slaves they own

41

represented a small fraction of the total slave population. Eli Faber, a historian of New York City's John Jay College, reported that in 1790, Charleston Jews owned a total of 93 slaves and that "perhaps six Jewish families" lived in Savannah in 1771.

Many wealthy Jews were also involved in the slave trade in the Americas, some as ship-owners who imported slaves and others as agents who resold them. In the United States, Isaac Da Costa of Charleston, David Franks of Philadelphia, and Aron Lopez of Newport, Rhode Island, are among the earliest American Jews who were prominent in the importation and sale of African slaves. In addition, some Jews were involved in the trade in various European Caribbean colonies. Alexandre Lindo, a French-born Jew who became a wealthy merchant in Jamaica in the late 18th century, was a major seller of slaves on the island.

This article goes on to make the argument that yes, Jews owned slaves, and yes, they were in the slave business; however, they were not the only ones, and certainly, they were, at best, small players; most importantly, Jews did not dominate the slave business.

This article was in response to a book published by the Nation of Islam in 1991. The book: *The Secret Relationship between Blacks and Jews, Volume One,* claims that Jews owned slaves "disproportionately more than any other ethnic or religious group in world history." The *My Jewish Learning* article and many other articles and books by Jewish scholars, historians, educators, and writers, widely condemned the Nation of Islam's book as being totally anti-Semitic. Jews vehemently criticized the book claiming it employed shoddy scholarly methods, cherry-picked information, relied on secondary historical accounts, had an incomplete index, and its footnotes were extremely difficult to check.

Of course, the book, *"The Secret Relationship between Blacks and Jews, Volume One,"* was anti-Semitic. It was meant to be an indictment of the Jews for their involvement in the slave business, that is, the owning, using, buying, and selling of African men, women, and children. What is interesting is that this book covers many things about the horrors of the African slave trade that are discussed in the New York Times Magazine issue on The 1619 Project. Yet, in the New York Times Magazine, the discussion is framed to convince the reader that it was only all white Christian men who were the villains of the African slave business. There is not one word about Jewish involvement in this evil business.

There is no secret about Jewish involvement in the slave business. Jewish scholars, historians, and writers have documented Jewish involvement in slavery in considerable detail. Eli Faber, in his book, *"Jews, Slaves, and the Slave Trade, Setting The Record Straight,"* lays out in great detail the research, data, and documentation that exists on Jews and slavery. The thrust of Faber's book, like many other Jewish writers on this topic, is that, yes, the Jews were involved in the slave business, but they were very small players and had little impact on the overall history of the African slave trade. Faber goes on to point out the many countries and nationalities were involved in this evil business, including the Portuguese, Spanish, Dutch, French, British, Danes, Swedes, German, and others. However, Faber fails to mention that Jews lived among all these peoples and certainly participated with their Christian neighbors in the slave business.

Even though Jewish scholars and writers have well documented Jewish involvement in the slave business, this history is almost unknown to the general public. Why? Quite simply because Jewish involvement in the slave business is not taught in American schools, discussed in the news media, or brought up in political debates or discussions about racism.

Nevertheless, in America, from 1654 to the end of the Civil War, Jews bought, sold, owned, and used African slaves. Sephardic Jews tended to be the most active in this business, and many of these Jews lived in the Southern states with major communities in Richmond, Charleston, and New Orleans, and smaller communities in other Southern cities and towns. Why did Sephardic Jews, in particular, come to America and engage in the slave business? The answer has to do with the rise of Russian power and the decline of the Ottoman Empire.

In the 18th century, Russia grew significantly as a European power and expanded its military capability on land and sea. Russia engaged Turkey in a series of wars between 1768 and 1774, slowly grinding down the Ottoman Empire. In 1776, the armies of Catherine the Great attacked Crimea, captured the fortress at Perekop, and began an occupation of the Crimean Peninsula. Russia's invasion and occupation put an end to Crimean Tatar slave raids into Russia, Poland, and Ukraine, and it drove the Rabbanite and Karaite Jews out of the slave business. As a result, the Ottoman Empire lost its supply of Christian Slavic slaves, and the Sephardic slave trader guild in Constantinople and other cities were effectively put out of business.

The loss of revenue from the slave business was, for the Ottoman Empire, one of the critical factors that contributed to the decline of its economy, its way of life, and its power. By the same token Sephardic Jews could not live the prosperous lifestyle they had for some 200 years in the Ottoman Empire; hence, they sought other areas for their livelihood. The slave trade to Brazil and the British colonies in the Americas was most attractive, so Sephardic Jews began to leave the Ottoman Empire and migrate to these new areas of opportunity.

Initially, American Jews in the North and South owned slaves; however, between 1777 and 1804, the Northern states ended slavery; nevertheless, Northern Jews still supported Southern Jewish ownership of slaves. Why would Jews, who throughout their history, suffered discrimination and subjugation be involved in the slave business? One reason is surprising; it has to do with the Bible.

The Torah recognizes the existence of slaves and defines two categories of slaves: the slave for life and the indentured slave. Typically, prisoners of war were enslaved, and they could be bought, sold, and used as their owners saw fit. Indentured slaves were those who had to work to pay off a debt. For centuries, Jewish moneylenders and others used indentured slaves as one way of getting payment from those who had defaulted on their loans. Since the Torah did not prohibit slavery, many Jews, up until slavery was outlawed in the 19th century, felt justified in pursuing the slave business. It is well documented that before and during the Civil War, rabbis and Jewish political leaders in both the North and the South gave impassioned speeches in defense of slavery.

For example, Rabbi Morris Raphall of New York's Congregation B'nai Jeshurun gave a sermon titled, "A Bible View of Slavery." In his sermon, Rabbi Raphall declared that "slavery has existed since the earliest time, slavery is no sin, and slave property is expressly placed under the protection of the Ten Commandments." Some rabbis rejected this interpretation of the Bible and insisted because a particular practice was condoned in the Bible did not make it right for modern times. Jewish rabbis had many passionate debates as to whether slavery was a moral evil or not.

However, the real motivation for pursuing the slave business was profit and the lifestyle that this business would provide for Jews. Bonnie K. Goodman writing in her paper the *"Confederacy safe haven for American Jews,"* states that American Jews found an oasis in the antebellum and Civil War South, free of anti-Jewish prejudice that was prevalent in the North at that time. Part of the reason was that American Jews joined and found common ground with Southern white Christians and partook in every aspect of Southern life, the good, the bad, slavery, racism, and participated in every aspect of the Civil War on the side of the South and the Confederacy.

In her paper, Goodman cites the writings of many Jewish scholars that seem to emphasize the main reason Southern Jews participated in slavery in the South was that they were free of anti-Semitism that existed in the North. Frankly, this view is overstated because even though Jews as new immigrants faced discrimination as did all-new immigrants, discrimination against Jews was rather benign compared to the blatant hatred and discrimination that Irish Catholics endured.

Irish Catholics could only survive by taking the dirtiest jobs, the most dangerous jobs, and the lowest-paying jobs. Hence, it was the Irish Catholic that worked in the coal mines, dug the canals, built the railroads, and cleared the swamps. Jews did not engage in these dangerous and back-breaking jobs; instead, they became peddlers, merchants, moneylenders, and entrepreneurs. On the whole, Jews had little or no problems pursuing a decent livelihood. In fact, during the Civil War years, Northern Jews obtained numerous lucrative government contracts to provide all sorts of materials to the Union Army.

The simple truth is that Jews in the antebellum South adapted and conformed to the Southern Christian lifestyle because they wanted to share in the wealth and privileges of this elite society. Just as the Ashkenazi Jews in the Polish-Lithuanian Commonwealth mirrored the lifestyle of the Polish nobles, and as the Sephardic Jews in the Ottoman Empire emulated the values, morals, and lifestyle of the ruling Muslims, Southern Jews, as historian Mark I Greenberg points out, adapted to the Southern way of life, including the code of honor, dueling, slavery, and Southern notions about race and states' rights.

Because of their extensive history in the slave business, the Sephardic Jews quickly adapted to the Southern social norms and values and assimilated without difficulty into Southern society. These Jews owned plantations and slaves and became slave traders, merchants, and political leaders in their communities. Thus, the Sephardic Jews obtained what they valued most--wealth, prestige, and political recognition. To the Jews at this time, the South was the land of Canaan where milk and honey flowed.

Christian and Jewish residents of the antebellum South fashioned a culture and a lifestyle that was unique and vastly different from that of Americans in the North. Plantation owners, in particular, saw themselves as descendants of English aristocrats, a race of gentlemen, with the dress, manners, and a code of honor that set them apart from residents of the North.

As time went on, Sephardic Jews integrated into the Christian society and became much like them; intermarriages became common, and Jewish religious obligations became secondary; yes, they were Jews, but they were, for the most part, not religious. Jewish family life changed as they adapted the morals, values, and norms of the Southern gentlemen. As the Sephardic Jewish men in the Ottoman Empire kept slave concubines for their sexual pleasure, Southern Jewish and Christian men had at their disposal female African slaves. Sexual relations between Southern men and African female slaves were well known in the South but never discussed; however, the population increases in light-skinned African slaves was obvious. Some Southerners even argued that breeding light-skinned slaves was good for the economy because lighter-skinned slaves could command a higher price.

Southern women lived and adapted to the reality of their life, much as Jewish wives did across the Ottoman Empire. These women could not have been happy to know that their sons and husbands were fornicating with slaves, but they accepted the practice without much resistance. Of course, the female African slave was in no position to complain or resist. By adapting to the Southern Christian way of life, Jews obtained political recognition, social acceptance, wealth, and security.

A good example of how far a Jew could rise in the Southern hierarchy was Juda Benjamin. Benjamin was born to Sephardic Jews from London. His parents were of modest means that moved several times seeking economic opportunities; around 1821, they finally settled in Charleston, South Carolina.

From an early age, it was obvious that Benjamin was extremely smart; in 1825, at age 14, Benjamin entered Yale College, but he left before he graduated, and no one knows why. Benjamin's life is shrouded in mystery because before he died, he destroyed all his papers. Most of what we know about his life comes from secondary sources and fragments of documents remaining after the Civil War. A few things are certain: Benjamin moved to New Orleans, Louisiana in 1828, became a clerk in a law firm, where he worked and studied as an apprentice.

In New Orleans, Benjamin met a fiery young woman named Natalie Bauche de St. Martin from a wealthy French Creole family. In 1833 Benjamin married Natalie, and she brought with her a dowry of $3000 and two young female slaves worth about another $1000. The marriage was stormy and troublesome for most of Benjamin's life, and by the 1840s, Natalie Benjamin was living in Paris with the couple's only child, Ninette, who was raised as a Catholic although Benjamin had not converted to Catholicism. Natalie's dowry was the seed money that Benjamin needed to launch his career in law.

There was no doubt that Judah Benjamin was brilliant, energetic, and hard-working; all of this, coupled with his cheerful personality, enabled him to carve out a career in law, business, and government. In addition to a very successful Louisiana law practice, he developed a large sugar cane plantation worked by hundreds of slaves.

His plantation made him rich, and he produced what Khalil Gibran Muhammad in his New York Times Magazine article for The 1619 Project called "the White Gold that Fueled Slavery."

Benjamin entered politics to become a United States senator from Louisiana. He was very active in the political arena, and he met, socialized, and became friends with men at the highest level of the American government. He was an outspoken supporter of slavery and argued that citizens had a right to their property as guaranteed by the Constitution. Of course, as a Southerner, Benjamin believed that the slaves he had purchased were his personal property. Benjamin, along with other Southern senators, made many impassioned speeches to defend slavery.

At some point, Benjamin met the Secretary of War Jefferson Davis and his wife, Varina; they developed a warm relationship based on mutual interests. Jefferson

Davis recognized Benjamin's abilities, and when the Civil War broke out, he offered him the position as attorney general in the Confederate government; thus, Davis became the first chief executive in North America to appoint a Jew to his cabinet. Davis gave Benjamin increasingly important roles in the government, where he served as Secretary of War and then Secretary of State; Judah Benjamin thus became the number two man in the Confederate government. Judah Benjamin served Jefferson Davis and the Confederacy much as his Sephardic ancestors had, for hundreds of years, served the Polish nobles, the Crimean Tatars, and the Ottoman Turks.

Jews in the South supported the Confederacy with their loyalty, their money, and their lives to maintain slavery. Upwards of 10,000 Jews joined the Confederate Army while some 6000 Jews in the North joined the Union Army. The actual numbers of Jews serving in the Confederate Army are debatable since many Confederate records were destroyed or lost after the war.

What is surprising is that many of the Jewish volunteers that joined the Confederate armies were latecomers to the South; they were the poor cousins of the Sephardic Jews, Ashkenazi Jews from Eastern Europe.

After the 1648 Cossack rebellion, the Polish-Lithuanian Empire began to decline in power and wealth. By 1795, Russia conquered the Polish-Lithuanian Empire, partitioned the country between Prussia, Austria, and Russia, and eliminated Poland from the map of Europe for more than 120 years. As the fortunes of the Polish nobles diminished, so did the wealthy lifestyle of the Ashkenazi Jews. Russia, in particular, erased many of the privileges that the Ashkenazi Jews had enjoyed under the Polish nobles; over time, these Jews became as poor as the serfs they had exploited for centuries.

For the Ashkenazi Jews, a particularly evil Russian edict was that Jews had to serve in the Russian army alongside all the other Slavic peoples in Russia's domain. At that time, service in the Russian army was for 25 years. Most Jews cried out, "My God, I will never see my son again, and they will make him become a Christian." Thus, Ashkenazi Jews started to migrate to the four corners of the world, with the United States being a popular destination.

Ashkenazi Jews who immigrated to the Southern states and compared their lives to that of Eastern Europe were delighted to find that they could earn their livelihoods as peddlers, shopkeepers, and entrepreneurs without interference and minimum anti-Semitism; also, they could vote like ordinary citizens, and as white, faced little or no discrimination. When the Civil War broke out, they expressed their desire to support their new country and volunteered to join the Confederate Army.

In his book, "*The Jewish Confederates*," Robert N. Rosen gives a detailed account of Jewish participation in the Confederacy during the American civil war of 1861 – 1865. The book covers well-known Southern Jews like Judah Benjamin, who supported the Confederate cause to protect their wealth, power, and prestige. The book also describes the lives of the more recent Southern Jews who did not own slaves or play a significant role in Southern politics. Rosen, as well as other Jewish authors, attempts to explain why these people from Eastern Europe joined the army to fight for the South. One of the main arguments or justifications used by many Jewish authors is that Southern Jews of all social levels fought for the South because the South was free from anti-Semitism. When times were good, there may have been minimal anti-Semitism in the South; however, when the war started to go bad for the South, anti-Semitism reared its ugly head with a vengeance.

After a string of losing battles and increases in shortages of food and supplies, the Ashkenazi Jews, in particular, were blamed for these problems. Because many of the Ashkenazi Jews spoke with a foreign accent and were small shopkeepers, the Christian Southerners saw them as moneygrubbing profiteers. Even well-established, high-level Jews like Judah Benjamin were blamed for the South's economic ills and military losses. The anti-Semitism that bubbled up in the South toward the end of the Civil War carried well into the 20th century.

In April 1865, the Union Army smashed into Richmond, Virginia; Jefferson Davis and his cabinet, including Benjamin, prepared to flee south. Benjamin packed his bags with as much gold as he could carry and joined Jefferson Davis and other cabinet members. After several days of traveling south, Jefferson Davis decided that he would go to Texas and try to continue the fight with the army that was still operational there. For his part, Benjamin headed south to Florida and, after many harrowing experiences, made his way to London, England.

In England, Benjamin became a barrister, and over time established a lucrative legal practice. Benjamin made his reputation among his peers through publications and was recognized for his brilliant mind. Benjamin worked at his law practice until his health failed him. While visiting his wife in Paris at the end of 1882, he suffered a heart attack, and his doctors ordered him to retire. Benjamin died on May 6, 1884; just before his death, he received the last rites of the Catholic Church and was interred at the Pere Lachaise Cemetery in the St. Martin family crypt.

Benjamin's grave did not bear his name until 1938 when a plaque was placed there by the Paris Chapter of the United Daughters of the Confederacy.

Southerners had made it clear from the beginning and throughout the Civil War that they were fighting to preserve their way of life and slavery. However, this narrative began to change after the South lost the war. The Daughters of the Confederacy, wives of Confederate generals, and numerous Southern writers and historians began to craft a new narrative and justification for the war. The new narrative about the Civil War emphasizes the South's desire to maintain states' rights and protect themselves from an invasion from the North by massive well-supplied armies made up of German and Irish mercenaries. This narrative was the basis for the "Myth of the Lost Cause," promoted after the South's defeat by Gen. Jubal Early and other Southern writers. These writers maintain that despite overwhelming odds, Gen. Robert E. Lee was the perfect product of the antebellum social system, and he towered above all other generals in ability and nobility. This myth was promoted for many years throughout the South, and organizations such as the Daughters of the Confederacy worked tirelessly to erect Confederate monuments and establish state holidays for the birthdays of Southern leaders, generals, and soldiers.

In today's era of the "Black Lives Matter" movement, many of these Civil War monuments are being torn down.

Chapter 5

The New York Times and The 1619 Project

Why did the New York Times in its 1619 Project not report on Jewish involvement in the slave business? The history of Jews and slavery is well documented, especially of Jews in the antebellum South before and during the Civil War. One reason may be that The New York Times has been owned and run by a Jewish family, the Ochs-Sulzberger family, for more than 125 years, and this family has a legacy of involvement in the slave business. They were slave owners and supported slavery before and during the Civil War.

Michael Goodwin, in his article "Why New York Times Praises 'Cancel Culture' but skips over its own racist history," reports that the Ochs-Sulzberger family supported slavery and the Southern cause and included family members who fought in the Confederate Army and contributed money to confederate memorials.

Furthermore, Goodwin goes on to report that the Times published articles that were sympathetic to the Southern cause, including a glowing profile of Jefferson Davis, the president of the Confederacy during the Civil War. Ochs family members belonged to the United Daughters of the Confederacy and had their names engraved on the founders' roll of the Stone Mountain Confederate Memorial in Georgia.

The Ochs family also helped fund Confederate cemeteries in Tennessee, Confederate veterans reunions, and the Chickamauga and Chattanooga National Military Park. When Ochs died, the United Daughters of the Confederacy sent a pillow embroidered with the Confederate flag to be placed in his coffin.

Certainly, no one likes to have the skeletons in their family dragged out for public view. Jews, in particular, are sensitive to any discussions about their involvement in the slave business. The ghost of anti-Semitism hangs over the head of every Jew; thus, Jews work hard to suppress any discussion that might be the basis for anti-Semitism. However, censoring discussions about Jews and slavery is a mistake because it will only generate conspiracy theories about the Jews.

In the last decade, there has been a significant rise in anti-Semitism in the United States and overseas. Conspiracy theories about Jews using their wealth to take over the world have existed since the publication of "The Protocols of the Learned Elders of Zion," in Russia in the early 1900s. The shooting at a Pittsburgh synagogue was by a young man who believed that the Jews are trying to take over the world; hate crimes are on the rise, and attacks on synagogues and individual Jews have reached record levels. The only way to fight conspiracy theories and hate speech is through transparency, honesty, and education.

The Times 1619 Project certainly failed to address Jewish involvement in slavery, but the Times' real failure is that it presented a narrow, selective, and biased view of slavery. The Times 1619 Project did not talk about the slavery inflicted on white Christian Slavic men, women, and children. The slavery of Christian Slavic people that existed for hundreds of years across the Polish-Lithuanian Commonwealth, the Crimean Tatar Peninsula, and the Ottoman Empire is older, larger, and more brutal than the African slave trade to America. The history of the Slavic slave trade needs to be remembered, understood, and presented forcefully, clearly, and honestly to inform and educate the American public.

Certainly, in the United States today, tens of thousands of African-Americans are descended from slaves; however, at the same time, there are tens of thousands of Christian Slavic Americans who are also descended from slaves. If there will be any serious discussion about slave reparations, then certainly Christian Slavic Americans must be part of this discussion. Every American needs to know and understand why the word Slav means slave.

References

Introduction

The New York Times, "The 1619 Project," *The New York Times Magazine,* August 2019.

David Marcus, "The New York Times Correction to the 1619 Project Proves it is not fit for Schools," *The Federalist,* March 13, 2020.

17th Century Poland and the Ashkenazi Jews

Chirovsky, Nicholas, *An Introduction to Ukrainian History, volume 2.* New York: Seton Hall University (1984).

Davies, Brian L., *Warfare, State and Society on the Black Sea Steppe,* 1500-1700. New York: Routledge (2007).

Davies, Norman, *God's Playground: A History of Poland.* New York: Columbia University Press (1982).

Gordon, Linda, *Cossack Rebellions.* Albany, NY: State University of New York Press (1983).

Graetz, Heinrich, *History of the Jews, volume 5.* Philadelphia, PA: The Jewish Publication Society of America, (1895).

Khodarkovsky, Michael, *Russia's Steppe Frontier, The Making of a Colonial Empire, 1500-1800.* Bloomington, Indiana: Indiana University Press, (2004).

Nathan Hanover, *Abyss of Despair.* New Brunswick, New Jersey: Transaction Publisher (2009).

Magocsi, Robert P., *A History of Ukraine.* Toronto: University of Toronto Press Inc. (1996).

Magocsi, Robert P., *Ukraine, an Illustrated History*. Toronto: University of Toronto Press (2007).

Rosamund, M. J., *The Lords' Jews*. Cambridge, Massachusetts: Harvard University (1990).

Subtelny, Orest, *Ukraine a History*. Toronto: University of Toronto Press Inc. (2009).

Wilson. Peter H., *The Thirty Years War, Europe's Tragedy*. Cambridge, Massachusetts: Harvard University Press (2009).

17th Century Crimea and the Rabbanite and Karaite Jews

Mike Dash, "Blond cargoes: Finish children in the slave markets of medieval Crimea," *A Blast From the Past*, January 2015.

Mikhail Kizilov, "Polish Slaves and Captives in the Crimea in the Seventeenth Century," *Acta Orientalia Hungaricae 73:2 (2020): 251-265*.

Mikhail Kizilov, "Reports of Dominican Missionaries as a Source of Information about the Slave Trade In the Ottoman and Tatar Crimea in the 1660s," *Journal: Acta Orientalia Academiae Scientiarum Hungaricae*, 2017.

Mikhail Kizilov, "Slaves, Money Lenders, and Prisoner Guards: The Jews and the Trade in Slaves and Captives in the Crimean Khanate," *Journal of Jewish Studies: Vol. LVIII, No. 2, Autumn*, 2007.

Mikhail Kizilov, "Slave Trade in the Early Modern Crimea from the Perspective of Christian, Muslim, and Jewish Sources," *Journal of Early Modern History 11(1-2):1-31*, March 2007.

Mikhail Kizilov, "The Karaites of Theodosia according to descriptions of travelers and some other written sources from the fifteenth to the nineteenth centuries," *Simferopol-Feodosia*, 2018.

Mikhail Kizilov, "The Black Sea and the Slave Trade: The Role of

Crimean Maritime Towns in the Trade in Slaves and Captives in the Fifteenth to Eighteenth Centuries," *The International Journal of Maritime History (IJMH)*, 2005.

Mikhail Kizilov, "The Crimean Karaites in the Portrayal of the 19th-century Polish travelers," *Brill*, January 2003.

17ᵗʰ Century Ottoman Empire and the Sephardic Jews

Alan W. Fisher, "The sale of slaves in the Ottoman Empire: markets and state taxes on slave sales, some preliminary considerations," *Begeri Bilimler – Humanities Vol. 6*, 1978.

Alan W. Fisher, "The Crimean Tatars," *Hoover Press*, 1987.

Alan W. Fisher, "The Russian Annexation of Crimea," *Cambridge University Press*, 1978.

Alan W. Fisher, "Muscovy and the Black Sea Slave Trade," *Canadian-American Slavic Studies*, 1972.

Alan W. Fisher, "The Ottoman Crimea in the Sixteenth Century," *Harvard Ukrainian Studies*, 1981.

Alan W. Fisher, "Emigration of Muslims from the Russian Empire in the Years after the Crimean War," *Jahrbücher für Geschichte Osteuropas*, 356-371, 1987.

Alan W. Fisher, "Chattel slavery in the Ottoman Empire," *Slavery and Abolition*, 1980.

Barnavi, Eli, *A Historical Atlas of the Jewish People*. New York: Schocken Books (1992).

Brownworth, Lars, *Lost to the West*. New York: Crown publishers (2009).

Crowley, Roger, *Constantinople*. London: Faber and Faber Ltd. 2005

Crowley, Roger, *Empire of the Sea.* London: Faber and Faber Ltd. 2008

Crowley, Roger, *Conquerors.* London: Faber and Faber Ltd. 2015

Yaron Ben-Naeh, "Blond, tall, with honey-colored eyes: Jewish ownership of slaves in the Ottoman Empire," *Springer Science Business Media,* 2006

17th Century American Jews

Barnavi, Eli, *A Historical Atlas of the Jewish People.* New York: Schocken Books (1992).

Ben Sales, "A California synagogue memorialize Judah Benjamin, the Confederacy's most prominent Jew. Here's how that change." *my Jewish learning,* 2002- 2020.

Bertram W. Korn, "The Jews of the Confederacy," *American Jewish Archives,* April 1961.

Bonnie K. Goodman, "The Confederacy safe haven for American Jews," *Unpublished thesis, McGill University,* June 2015.

David Brian Davis, "Jews and the slave trade," *the Baltimore Sun,* February 13, 1994.

Evans, Eli N., *Judah P. Benjamin, The Jewish Confederate.* New York: The Free Press (1988).

Faber, Eli, Jews, *Slaves, and the Slave Trade, Setting the Record Straight.* New York: New York University Press, (1998).

Hanover, Nathan, *Abyss of Despair.* New Brunswick (USA): Transaction Publishers (2009).

Jim Winnerman, "Jews in the Civil War," *Special to the Jewish light,* January 4, 2012.

Johnson, Paul, *A History of the Jews.* New York: Harper & Row,

Publishers (1987).

Lankiewicz, Don, *Journey to Asylum*. Needham, Mass: Donald Lankiewicz (2015).

Lev Meirowitz, Nelson, "Does the Bible condone slavery?" *my Jewish learning*, 2002-2020

Michael Feldberg, "George Washington's letter to Newport," *my Jewish learning*, 2002-2020

MJL Staff, "Jews and the African slave trade," *my Jewish learning, 2002-2020*.

MJL Staff, "Halacha: the laws of Jewish life," *my Jewish learning*, 2002-2020.

Norman H. Finkelstein, "Jews in the Civil War," *my Jewish learning*, 2002-2020

Rosen, Robert N., *The Jewish Confederates*. Columbia, South Carolina: University of South Carolina Press (2000).

Winthrop D. Jordan, "Slavery and the Jews," *the Atlantic*, September 1995.

The New York Times and the 1619 Project

David Marcus, "The New York Times' Correction to the 1619 Project Proves it is not fit for Schools," *The Federalist*, March 13, 2020.

Ken Blackwell, "The New York Times' Dark History of Slave Ownership," *Townhall*, July 24, 2020.

Michael Goodwin, "Why New York Times praises "cancel culture," but skips over its own racist history: Goodwin, *The New York Post*, July 11, 2020.